A Cup of Wisdom

WITH

a Shot of Sarcasm

A Cup of Wisdom

WITH

a Shot of Sarcasm

ROBERT H. MA

A CUP OF WISDOM: WITH A SHOT OF SARCASM

Cover images by Allen Lee.
Interior images created by Alfred Hernandez.
Cover and interior design by Ezra Barany

Published by Barany Publishing

ISBN: 978-0-9904087-0-3

Printed in the U.S.A.

Acknowledgments

I would like to thank the editors Ezra & Beth Barany for their patience, insights and guidance. I also would like to thank Alfred Hernandez for his beautiful illustrations for this book.

To my family, partners and friends with whom I probably wouldn't have much to write about, thank you for your encouragement.

To my beautiful wife, Ana Ma, thank you for putting up with all my wisecracks. Thank you for your critiques for keeping my quotes honest. Thank you for keeping my heart young and my spirit true.

I would like to thank my daughter Courtney Ma, the girl I called my little detective, and now my little philosopher. Thank you for letting me run all these quotes by you without you getting bored.

Last but not least, to all my wonderful customers, thank you for your inspiration, your wisdom and your stories, and for your continuing support.

Introduction

Our subconscious is uninhibited. It will explore without your permission. It dares to go where you are unwilling. It has an insatiable appetite. It has no boundaries, no limits, only the ones you acknowledge.

Your subconscious can be your teacher, a friend or your enemy. It can help you cope with your daily frustration. At night, it manifests itself in your dreams. At times we wake up sobbing because in this society we are taught to be strong, not to show our emotions. But our subconscious doesn't know that. It has no rules. One of its purposes is to protect.

Even though you don't know its limits, it knows yours.

It can take you to different dimensions. It does not sleep. It's 24/7 like a pilot light that never goes out. Your subconscious is where all your creativity lies. – Find a way to tap into it.

Every one of us can be brilliant.

The journey is to connect with your subconscious.

~Rob

Peer pressure is like an invisible gun, the trigger is the emotion, the bullet is the consequence.

Confucius says,
"Keep your chin up…
but beware of dog shit."

Give a man a bird and he will eat for a day. Teach him how to shoot and he will become a Republican.

It is good to lose one's temper, just don't be foolish looking for it again.

Ordinary people have five senses. If you are lucky, you will have six. If you are *really* lucky you'll make no sense at all and become a politician.

If talk is cheap, then why the hell is my cell phone bill so high?

Confucius says, "The secret to staying young is to stay away from mirrors."

Home invasion is when your in—laws come over but un—invited.

Common sense should
be so common that
it's uncommon
not to have any.

Elvis's favorite sandwich was peanut butter and banana. What was Bruce Lee's favorite sandwich?

How can we stand on solid ground when the earth itself is suspended?

The art of fighting without
fighting is when
I pay someone to
kick your ass.

I'm struggling to struggle
with whatever I'm
struggling with.

But during my struggle, I
have learned things that I
might not have been able to
learn if not for my struggle.

The key is to snuggle
– and not knuckle –
with your struggle.

The greatest treasure on earth is the one buried inside your head.

The meaning of life is to continue to find its meaning.

Failure is a bitter pill to swallow…especially if it's self–prescribed.

Comedians are the greatest philosophers. They can take a horrible situation and turn it into a funny situation, and a funny situation into an even funnier situation. They dare to laugh at everything and everyone, including themselves. Now that's the ultimate philosopher.

Forgetting your morals
will not lead you to
a better tomorrow.

Success is not measured by how much money you make, but by how much you give; otherwise, Ghandi and Mother Teresa would have been seen as failures.

Hope is thought without action. One can hope, but nothing will happen.

You can't fully digest someone's culture without digesting their food.

Ugly is not what we see,
it's what we are.

Forgive and forget. I say, forget period. Then you have nothing to forgive.

An alchemist is someone that can turn metal into gold. But a true alchemist can turn gold into worthless metal.

Without love, a home
is like a shell
without its pearl.

There's no struggling
in quitting.

It's very difficult to say goodbye in the physical world, but in a spiritual world, there are no goodbyes, because there is no end in eternity.

Without sorrow,
would we know what
happiness is?

The mirror is the birth of our ego and the beginning of our vanity.

Compassion is not to be taught but to be felt.

To keep an argument from escalating, simply change two words. From "You are" to "I am."

We cannot escape our
destiny in this world
for our salvation is
not of this world.

You can buy a mansion and fill it up with all kinds of things, but without love, your heart will remain empty.

In this society, we seem
to be fixated with
labels which separate
and divide us.

For instance, he is "black," he
is "white," he is "gay," he is
"straight,"…

If we do away with labels,
then what do we have left?
Just "is."

Let go of hate, or hate will not let go of you.

In relationships, it's okay
if your partner comes
with baggage...

It's the ones with carry—on
you should be aware of.

Stand up tall, even if you are short, for your adversary will meet you eye–to–eye when they fall.

Life is like a maze. It has many twists and turns. Sometimes you find yourself repeating the same path; occasionally, you'll hit a dead–end, but if you stay focused, and work hard, you will turn a "maze" into something amazing.

If seeing is believing, then hearing must be gossip.

High hopes will keep gravity from pulling us down.

If someone slaps your
right cheek, turn and offer
them your left cheek; if they
slap your left cheek, then
turn and offer them
your butt cheek.

Seeing smoke is never good…unless it's from a joint. Then it's *allll* good.

Grass is greener on the other side, until you hop the fence and discover it's astro–turf.

A happy meal is when your friend picks up the tab after dinner.

"Vegetarians are regular people," my mom says. "If you eat your veggies, you'll be regular too."

What is Zen?

I don't know Zen,
so I make no Zen.

Tripping is when you're vacationing from your mind; just don't make it a permanent one.

I've been told many times I do things half–ass, so my goal is to be a complete ass.

Censorship to an artist
is like asking them to
paint you a rainbow
but without color.

A thirst for learning and an appetite for knowledge is good, but monitor what you consume, be careful what you digest. Constipation of the mind can make you a shithead.

If you think in circles, then
you're not thinking
outside the box.

The worse kind of failure
is fear of failure. As long as
you try, success then becomes
nothing but a process of
elimination.

Knowledge is power.
It can provide you with
enough ammunition to
shoot down all the lies
in this world.

We might not understand
each other's language,
but we can seek to
understand each other
through kindness.

In relationships it's not important what your significant other does for a living. It doesn't matter how much he or she makes. What is important is inspiration. If you can't inspire, then the relationship will soon expire.

The heart is the anchor
that keeps us from drifting.

Keys to the piano are
separated by black and white,
the key to harmony is to
combine the two to create
a colorful sound.

People that love money
will never love people.
People that love people
will never love money.

To combat greed is to stop the desire in excess. Then we will have less desire for money.

We can't change the past, but if we don't move forward, we can't change the future either.

People that are blinded
by their own needs will
never see yours.

Beauty is in the eye of the beholder. But don't blame the eyes for what the heart sees.

If a stranger slaps you
it's humiliation. If your
parent slaps you it's discipline.
When God slaps you it's
a wake–up call.

When you're met with a challenge, do you perspire or are you inspired?

Fake love must be easy if
true love is hard to find.

There are plenty of fish in the sea, but the one that swims alone is the "selfish."

It was curiosity that killed the cat, but it was also curiosity that lead him to the secret of nine lives.

To practice, "see no evil, hear no evil," just pretend someone is yelling at you in a dark room and in a language you don't understand.

There are those who
think and those who
think they think, if you are
those who think they think,
then you're not thinking,
because thinking should
be effortless.

We don't hate you because you're beautiful; we hate you because your personality is ugly.

If all we do is take and never give back, soon this world will be an empty space.

If you're someone who likes to wait until the new year to make a New Year's resolution, that's not really a resolution, it sounds more like procrastination.

It's funny how most
of us have a hard time
remembering people's
names, but have no problem
calling each other names.

Nice guys finish last,
so find yourself a nicer guy,
so you won't have to.

Life is about looking forward (not backward). Otherwise, our creator would have given us eyes in the back of our heads. Flies have eyes in the back of their head, but they also have nothing to look forward to. That's why they eat shit.

The art of thinking
without thinking is when
you are on autopilot.

If the letter "J" in Spanish is pronounced like the letter "H" in English, then my friend Joe is actually a hoe?

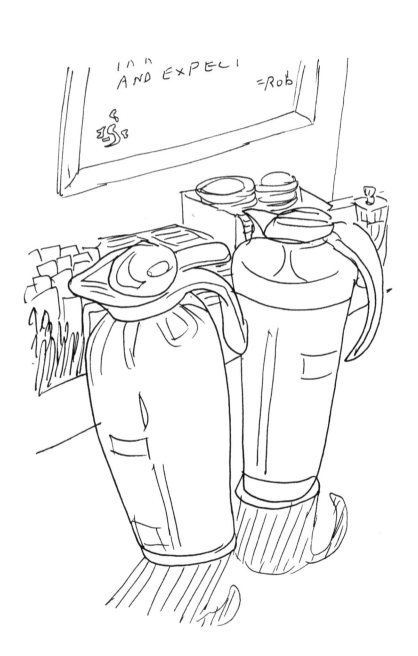

On Spare the Air Day, please refrain from eating beans.

If you think "No pain, no gain" is about building muscle, it's not. It's about building a fortune. Just ask the pharmaceutical companies.

If you want to fantasize about your fortune go see a fortune teller. If you want to know the truth about your fortune, go see your bank teller.

Fear is not always our enemy, fear can be our ally. Otherwise, we would be jumping into water not knowing how to swim.

Superficial beauty will carry you a few decades. Inner beauty will last a lifetime.

Journey into the woods,
surrender to nature,
dissolve your ego and
become ecotistical.

Why do people get upset with name–calling? If it's not your name, why do you respond?

It's hard to get used to someone, but it's much easier to get used to one's self.

Life is a work of art. It's rich
in color, and it's the right
combination that makes
it a masterpiece.

Mistakes can be costly;
but learning from them
can be priceless.

The day might not be great,
but be grateful for the day.

Do not fall in love with
the face but with the
heart. The face has
many expressions,
the heart has only one.

Listen to the ocean. If you pay attention, the sound of the waves will carry a message of yesteryear.

True intelligence is
when one discovers
his own stupidity.

All bruises go away in a few days. Except for the bruises to our ego.

Die for money,
die for fame,
die for nothing,
what a shame.

Stars belong in the sky,
not on cement where
anyone can walk
all over you.

In a world of darkness, let faith be your guiding light.

To live is to learn
to participate with
everything in this world.
You can't shut yourself
out of either good or bad,
even if you try.

Memories Behind the Tree:

Trees have outlasted our ancestors and they will outlast us. Trees do not rely on us—we rely on them. When we go, trees remain, but when trees go, we go.

Which came first?
Knowledge or the book?
If knowledge came first, then
why do we need books? If
books came first, where did
knowledge come from?

Arrest the art, and you will arrest the heart.

There is no quality
without the "E" in equality.

The essence of happiness
is simplicity and gratitude.

Spirituality should never
be organized because spirits
are meant to be free.

They say love is blind because love is not seen but felt from the heart.

The meaning of life
cannot be found in a
dictionary because life
is not defined
by a book.

Not all times are equal. Good times will make time fly, and tough times will make you wise.

No matter how much money you have, you can't buy time, but you can sure spend a lot of it.

Temptation is great,
but the consequences
are even greater.

Striving for success is admirable, only if monetary reward is secondary.

In this society, we are given multiple masks. Which one you choose is entirely up to you, but choose wisely. The one you wear the most will one day become permanent.

One shit we wish we could flush away is "bullshit."

People like to say you only live once. If you only live once, then why do you want to f*&k things up?

I finally realized that my back pain wasn't due to lifting heavy objects, but by constantly bending over for the government.

If I sweat bullets,
whose son am I?

Son of a gun.

Love is a many—splendored thing, until a divorce wipes you out of everything.

A senior citizen discount?
What about a children's
discount? They're the
ones who haven't made
a dime yet.

You know you're vain if you start striking poses in a lightning storm.

Confucius says, "He who drinks from an empty cup will never spill on himself."

The best way to get rid of a cold is to give it to somebody else.

Pretend the world is blind
and charm us with your
personality and not
with your looks.

The apple does not fall far from the tree…unless the tree is planted on a hill.

There's no prescription
for short sightedness. Your
view will simply make a
spectacle of yourself.

What is the difference between pride and proud? Pride is having nothing yet willing to work hard for everything. Proud is having nothing, but sit on our ass and expect everything.

You'll need a head
in order to get ahead.

Life is nothing but a dream
because we dream at night
and daydream during the day.

If you are the type to always wait for the perfect moment, that moment might not ever come. The time you spent waiting, might have been the moment you were waiting for.

Love is about putting up with each other's flaws and not using them as weapons.

No matter how much
you love the mirror,
one day, the mirror is
going to betray you.

Duplicated minds will
lead us to destruction.
Individual minds will
lead us to freedom.

History will be history if we continue to cut education funding. More cuts to our music program and we'll be facing the music instead of playing it.

Being successful in business
doesn't guarantee you
success in life.

God shined his light upon
me to reveal my dark shadow.

Untitled

Her smile darkens the day,
but her pain glows in the
dark.

One hand pushes away death.
The other welcomes it.

Hands cannot teach love.
Love teaches love. Love is not
made of money; love is made
of kindness.

Your flesh might be bought,
but your soul is priceless.

You're only lost because the person who guides you has no moral compass. It's better to run away empty than to stay in a world full of lies.

Win at all costs, but not if it costs you your life.

Beauty without a heart is like a mirror without a reflection.

Would we recognize
salvation if there were
no suffering?

Physical attraction is
good. But you also
need spiritual connection
to find a soulmate.

I'll shoot for the moon, and I'll fly to the moon, then I will walk on the moon, but until then, I'll just gaze at the moon.

"Sticks and stones might break my bones, but words will never hurt me"… except break my spirit.

Trying to understand others is admirable, but seek to understand one's self first. If you don't, you won't understand others.

Do you see the glass
half empty or half full?

It depends on if I'm thirsty.

"Love is blind, but keep one eye open after marriage."

Scientists say the one thing that is constant is change. I agree.

If not for our mind, at least our underwear…

I should hope…

Love is allowing one's self to be a stepping–stone for the other. Then I realized that I'm the stone and you're the boulder.

In life, everyone has fallen down one time or another. But it's not how hard you fall, it's how hard you climb that defines you.

In leadership it's not how well you manage people, it's how well you manage emotion.

Violence is an airborne virus
—an epidemic that the
media loves to spread.

A beautiful day is not
in its appearance but in
it's nature.

We see with our eyes, but we dream with our heart.

I love to travel the world, but I don't always have the money. Then I realize we're in the San Francisco Bay Area, where the world travels to us.

There are no shortcuts in life. "Shortcut" only means you're cutting yourself short.

Why do we chase happiness? If happiness is within, then there is nothing to chase.

I have met a lot of
interesting people, but
none more interesting
than the one I met
in the mirror.

A world without music is a world without rhythm.

Focus on what you can do instead of focusing on what others should do.

Do not project red
in an argument.

God does not divide, we
—in the name of religion—
do the dividing ourselves.

Have passion at work, and you will be rewarded twice.

Parenthood is not defined by blood but by love.

If nothing bad happens in a day, then it's a good day.

If something good happens, then it's a great day.

The past makes way for the old. The old make way for the young. The young make way for the future.

You know the old saying,
"Don't work too hard?"
Don't take it too seriously
because you'll find yourself
working much harder in
your older age if you didn't
in your younger age.

Silent partners aren't always silent until you start making a profit.

Before marriage a man will lay down his life for you. After marriage, he'll just lie down all the time.

Is there a God? If there is no God, then we truly need a miracle.

Plastic surgery should only be performed on a credit card with a pair of scissors.

If someone constantly stabs you in the back, then it's time to start walking behind them.

In this world, since
we have no choice but
to live together, we
might as well enjoy
each other's company.

If life is a race,
then I want to finish last.

About the Author

Robert H. Ma was born in China, and has lived in Hong Kong. He immigrated to the U.S. with his mom and three of his six siblings. He now helps run a cafe, a family business in Oakland, California, and lives in Alameda with his wife and daughter. On his off–hours, he likes to exercise, spend time with his family, and read books on spirituality and philosophy.

Printed in Great Britain
by Amazon.co.uk, Ltd.,
Marston Gate.